MOMISMS
The Daily Struggle

DON'T LICK THAT!!

A Hilarious Adult Coloring Book on Motherhood for All the Stressed Out Mommies...Just Like Me

FREE DOWNLOADS

For your FREE Coloring Pages
Visit us at:

http://www.wordofmm.com/

YOUR DOWNLOAD CODE:
MOMLIFE

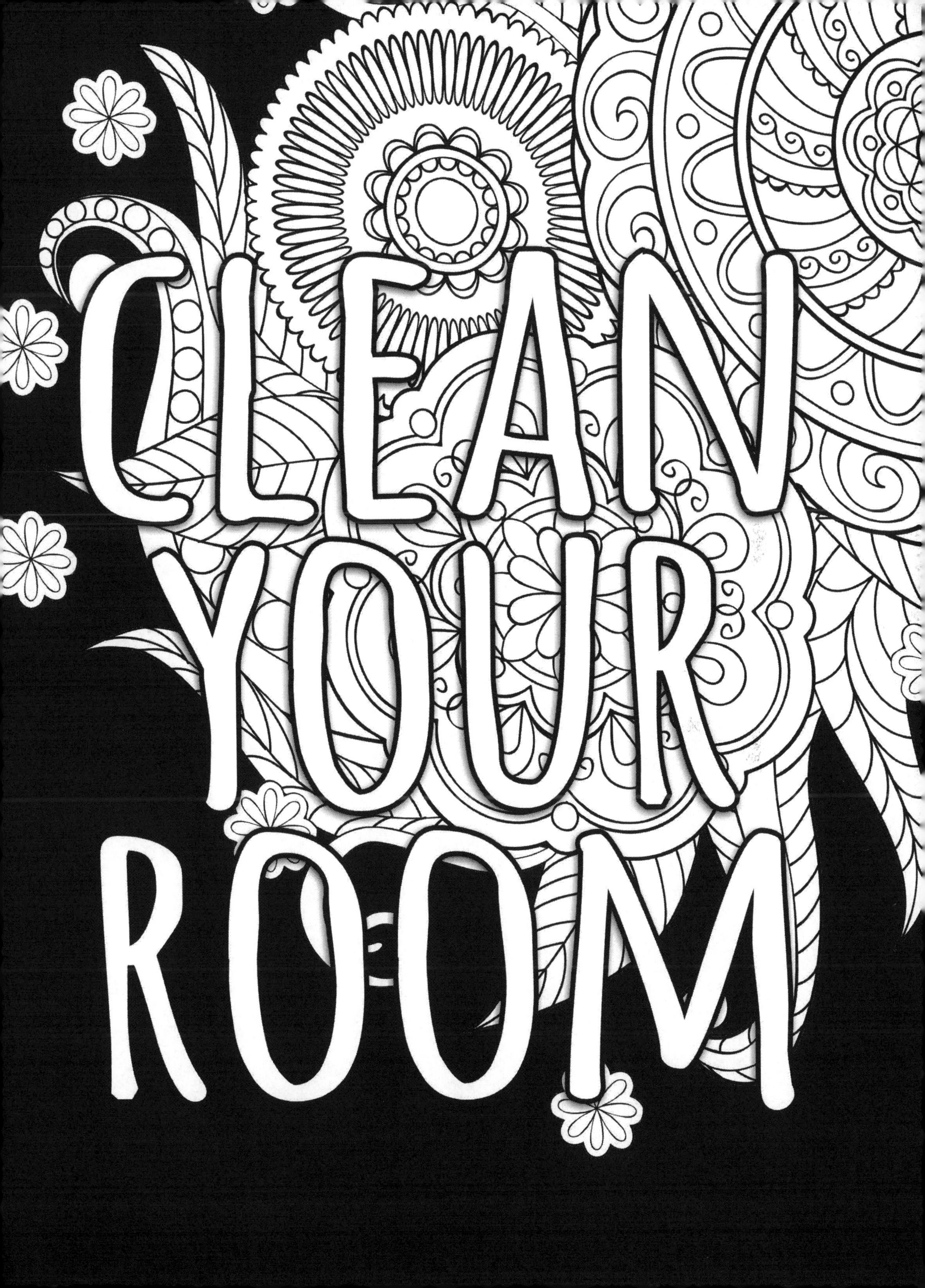
CLEAN
YOUR
ROOM

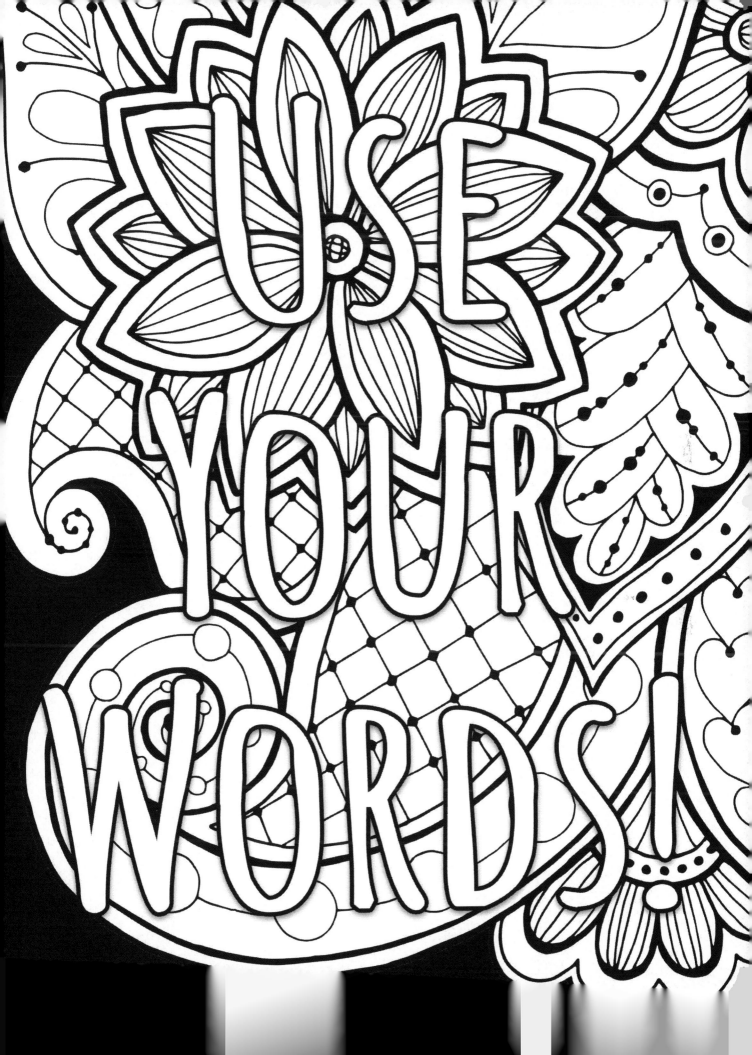

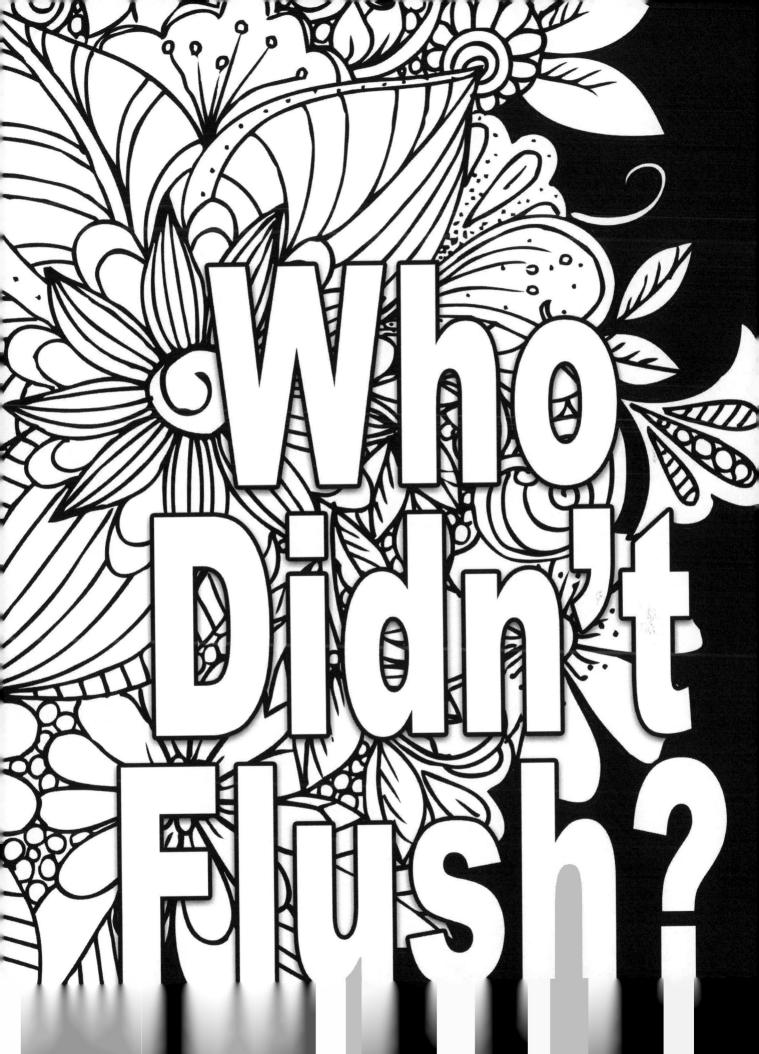

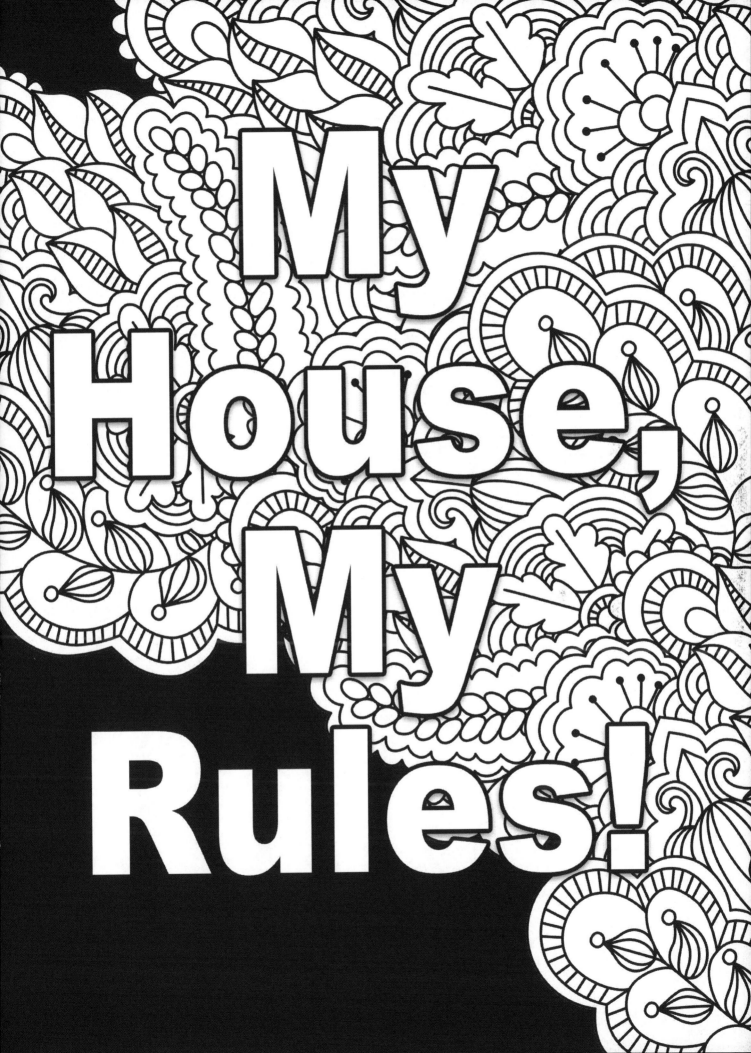

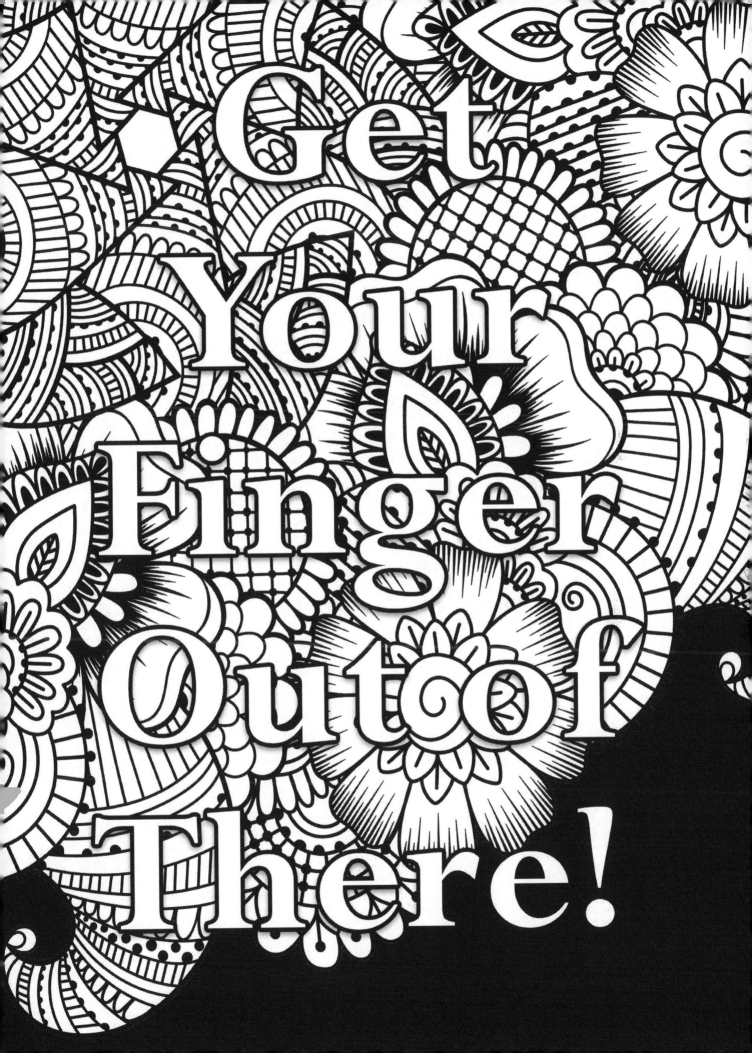

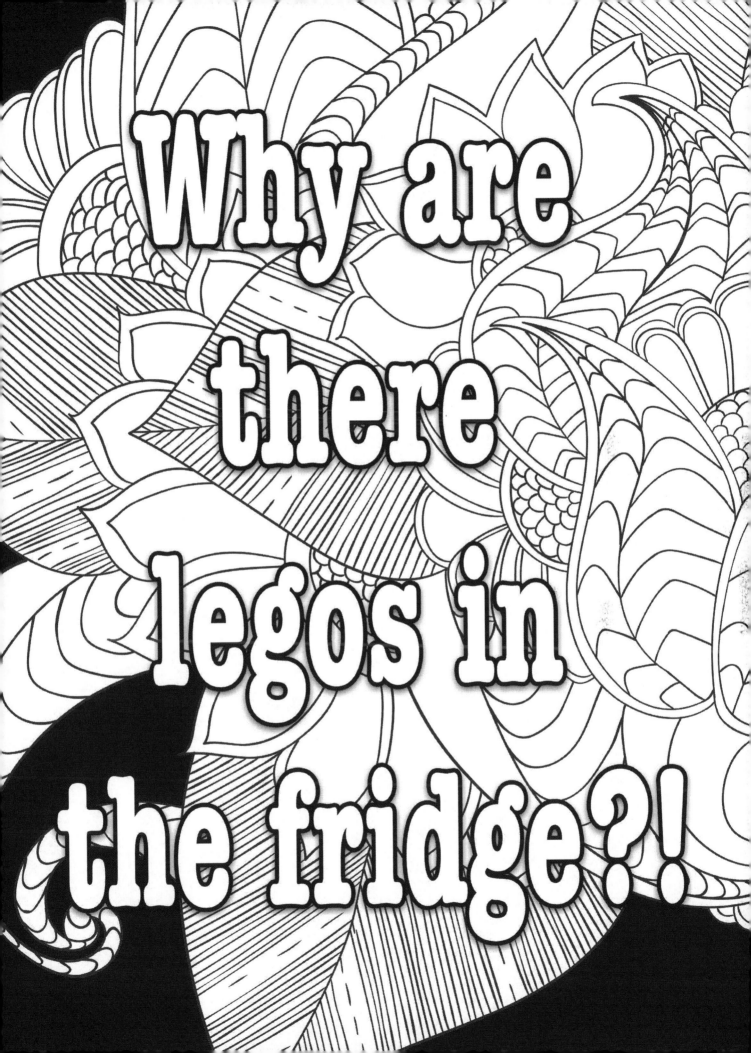